ON CUE
Helping children to read

For parents at home
and supporters in schools

PETER GUPPY and MARGARET HUGHES

A NASEN Publication

Published in 2003

© Peter Guppy and Margaret Hughes

ISBN 1 901485 65 X

The right of Peter Guppy and Margaret Hughes to be identified as authors of this work has been asserted by them in accordance with the Copyright, Designs and Patents Act 1988.

Published by NASEN.
NASEN is a registered charity. Charity No. 1007023.
NASEN is a company limited by guarantee, registered in England and Wales.
Company No. 2637438.

Further copies of this book and details of NASEN's many other publications may be obtained from the NASEN Bookshop at its registered office: NASEN House, 4/5 Amber Business Village, Amber Close, Amington, Tamworth, Staffs. B77 4RP.
Tel: 01827 311500; Fax: 01827 313005; Email: welcome@nasen.org.uk
Website: www.nasen.org.uk

Cover design by Mark Procter.
Typeset in Times by J. C. Typesetting and printed in the United Kingdom by Stowes, Stoke-on-Trent.

Contents

Acknowledgements

The authors would like to thank Janet Pilcher for all her help and support.

The authors and publisher wish to express their grateful thanks to the following for their permission to include extracts: A. P. Watt Ltd for *Saddlebottom*, by Dick King-Smith; Harcourt Educational for *Breakfast* from the Young Shorty series by James Webster; A & C Black for *Bumblebee* by Bo Jarner; Walker Books for *The Big Big Sea* by Martin Waddell, and *The Piggy Book* by Anthony Browne; Oxford University Press for *Castle Adventure* from the Oxford Reading Tree by Roderick Hunt; Hodder-Arnold for the extract by Sheila McCullough on pages 102-103 and 110. Every reasonable effort has been made to contact publishers. We apologise for any omissions which will be rectified in future editions of this book.

Note to schools

This book has been written to give Teaching Assistants and parents a greater insight into cueing strategies and how children learn to use them, in order that they might support you, the teacher, in your work.

We recognise that our exclusive focus on one-to-one interactions does not represent the classroom situation.

However, we have chosen this approach for two reasons:

- It does depict typical home settings.

- It allows us to provide focused, uncluttered descriptions of the learning process, clearly uncovering cueing strategies in action. These descriptions are intended to support parents and Teaching Assistants in following teachers' advice and instructions with a greater understanding, rooted in a shared knowledge base.

Moreover, all the techniques are transferable to group and class situations.

Introduction

The amount of time spent listening to children read at home and at school is considerable. But is it always time well spent?

This book aims to ensure that your time is indeed well spent, by providing you with the necessary insights into the world of teaching reading.

Answers are given to many frequently asked questions, such as:

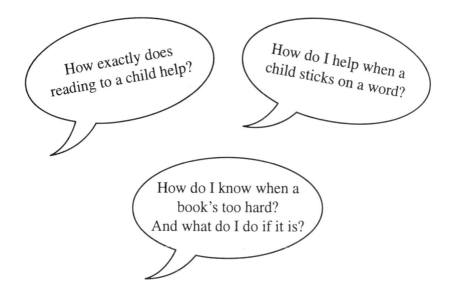

How exactly does reading to a child help?

How do I help when a child sticks on a word?

How do I know when a book's too hard? And what do I do if it is?

Technical terms are explained, and many short scenes are used to demonstrate just how much learning can take place when the adult talks knowledgeably with the reader while "hearing reading".

So get ready for your journey into reading development, which begins here in Chapter 1 at the beginning - HOW READING WORKS.

Chapter 1:
How reading works

This chapter aims to show you:

- **that reading works through cues;**

- **what cues are;**

- **where cues are to be found;**

- **how a reader uses cues.**

It will help you to:

- **recognise the two types of cue:**
  UNSEEN - cues in the reader's mind
  SEEN - cues on the page;

- **recognise that reading works through a balanced use of both.**

Turn over for Ben's balancing act.

Ben's balancing act

Meet Ben. Ben is nine, and through early support has built the good foundation he needs.

Let's watch him as he tackles a problem word in the central box below.

Because I know this is a ghost story, I'm expecting a word to do with ghosts.

Because the previous word is 'the', I'm expecting the word to be a noun ('the something-or-other')

The night was dark, without a moon and given to swirling fog, but he was not afraid as he entered the graveyard, feeling his way from headstone to headstone. As he reached the old chapel, it went colder. Then he saw it - the **phantom**, white and shadowy, with a faint green glow about it.

Yes, it's *phantom* all right. These next few words clinch it.

OK. It can't be *ghost* or *spirit* because it starts with *p*; it looks like *p-han-tom*. P-hantom? Pantom? Ah! *ph*, like 'Philip'. It's *ph-ant-om*.

Phantom! Like on my video!

8

The cues Ben used

Ben combined his knowledge of stories, language and ghosts with his knowledge of phonics to complete the puzzle. Background knowledge told him to expect a ghostly word, and phonic knowledge of "ph" clinched it for him.

He
BALANCED

what was in his mind

with

what was on the page.

Ben was successful in solving that problem because he made good use of "cues".

DETECTIVES LOOK FOR CLUES

READERS LOOK FOR CUES

Like Ben, successful readers balance two types of cue

> **UNSEEN**
> Cues that are in the reader's head.

> **SEEN**
> Cues that are on the page.

Neither type works alone.
Each has equal importance.
Each works in conjunction with the other.

 Now let's see what kinds of cues are to
be found within each type.

UNSEEN CUES: background knowledge - readers draw
upon their experience of:

- life in general;

- vocabulary;

- different kinds of reading materials ... *e.g. books, comics, poems, adverts*;

- different kinds of stories ... *e.g. fairy, horror, funny, adventure, fantasy*;

- different authors' voices ... *e.g. serious, jokey, friendly, formal*;

- book-language ... *e.g. 'at the far forest's edge', 'however long the road...'*.

SEEN CUES: the printed page - from which readers:

- recognise whole words;

- recognise letters, and groups of letters, and use them in the building of words;

- recognise punctuation;

- "read" pictures;

- use of context:
  both by using the general meaning of the page and by knowing how to sensibly complete a run of words,
  e.g. 'He took _____ gold to fill ten bags' [enough].

The part cues play when you read

As we've already said, detectives look for clues, but readers look for cues.

That's why the National Literacy Strategy places great importance on the use of cues.

It explains that the ability to "orchestrate a full range of reading cues" is a vital part of literacy.
(p.3, National Literacy Strategy Framework)

Every printed page is full of cues - the letters, the pictures, the order of the words, the overall topic.

And every reader has a fabric of cues within their own head, just waiting to be used.

This is why ...

… every adult helping children to read should become a cue spotter.

**Have a go at spotting the cues
Ben used to read _Thames_.**

In his guide book to London, Ben came to:
The Thames flows through the middle of London
He read: The _Th… Th-ames_ flows through the middle
of London:
(He pronounced _Th_ as in _thumb_, and _–ames_
as in _names_)
Ben: _Th-ames? What's that?_
Ben re-read the sentence to himself.
Ben: _Aaah!_ flows through… London! _It's that river!_
He now read: The Thames flows through the middle of
London.
[This time he pronounced it correctly as _Tems_]

So, which cues helped Ben recognise _Thames_?

The cues Ben used

With *Thames* coming so early in the sentence, it seemed that Ben had no cues other than the phonics of the word itself.

But these phonics were not very helpful. After all, *th* is not usually a *t* sound, and *ames* is not usually sounded as *ems*.

If he'd met *Trent* or even *Mississippi,* the phonic cues would have been more reliable.

However, he carried on and took in information from *flows through* and *middle of London,* which gave him more cues to draw on.

This allowed him draw on another important cue: his own general knowledge.

Once armed with the knowledge from all these cues, there was just enough phonic information in *T___m_s* to clinch it for him. (<u>And</u> to teach him a new spelling!)

Ben had made use of a variety of cues from different places, by:

- being confident enough to read on past a problem word to gather more information;

- using his general knowledge;

- making sensible use of phonics.

You can see, then, that if you are to be a useful supporter of children's reading, you need to help them get the benefit of as many cues as possible.

Remember! A cue can be more than one word.

As a cue-spotter, where will you find cues?

You will find cues…

1… just before the problem word
　　He looked at the clock to see the <u>time</u>.
The words *He looked at the clock* are a
strong cue for <u>time</u>.

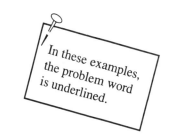

In these examples,
the problem word
is underlined.

2… just after the problem word
　　Bill <u>laughed</u>. *Hee hee hee.*
The rare phonics of <u>laughed</u> are immediately over-ridden by the cue
from those simple-to-read sounds of laughter.

3… some distance before the problem word
　　"What's that? You're covered in spots! *It's not catching, is it?*"
　　"*No, no.* I know you don't want your Leonard getting it. It were
　　bad enough when he had measles, chicken pox and whooping
　　cough. It's just an <u>allergy</u>," she said.
The cue *It's not catching, is it? … No, no* is presented several lines
before the word <u>allergy</u>.

4… some distance after the problem word
　　She lay there, very white, just <u>alive</u>.
　　"Take her to the castle and *tell the*
　　women to look after her."
This reader found no help in the picture, in which
the princess seems dead. But the words *tell the women to look after*
her provide the cue that she is still <u>alive</u>.

Remember!
"Some distance" can
be as much as several
pages away.

5... in the reader's own general knowledge
    Jupiter is the biggest of the planets.
Prior knowledge of the planets acted as a cue.

6... in a picture
    Titch and his tricycle.
A wonderful *illustration* provided a clear cue.

7... in the phonics of part of the problem word
    Lots of hard *mul*tiplication sums were set by the maths teacher.
The phonic building of *mul-* acted as the cue; it triggered the rest of the word.

8... in the phonics of the whole problem word
    This is a *cardinal* beetle.
Sometimes the problem word is not supported by any information from page, picture or the reader's general knowledge, other than the letters themselves. It may still be possible to read the word by building it, the letters themselves being the cues.

**These descriptions show where cues are to be found.
They show that the reader has to be prepared
to travel widely, back and forth, crossing full stops
and sometimes even pages, to find them.**

**They also show that...
ONE CUE IS NEVER ENOUGH**

One cue is never enough

For instance, take Example 8 from the previous page.

Lots of hard multiplication sums were set by the maths teacher.

The reader was stuck on *multiplication.*
He built the first syllable: *mul-.*
Then he used meaning cues, from *maths* and from *sums,* to clinch his reading of the word.
He started with phonic cues, and meaning cues clinched it.

And Example 6 on the previous page:

Jupiter is the biggest of the planets.

This reader already knew the names of several planets.
She brought in phonics to work alongside this knowledge.
She used the letters/sounds of the word *Jupiter* to select the correct planet from the rest of the possibles: Neptune, Pluto, Mars …
She started with meaning cues, and phonic cues clinched it.

Now meet Kate, Jack, Rosie and Harry

They are young readers who have reached a stage at which they can tackle problem words by themselves, using a balance of cues.

This balance is the "orchestration of cues" of which the National Literacy Framework speaks.

So let's watch these children as they each use a combination of cues to solve a problem word.

Kate:

"Do that again and you'll go <u>straight</u> to bed", said mum.
Straight was a tricky word for Kate, because she didn't know *aight*.
But she combined the cues *str* and *to bed* with another cue:
her personal knowledge of an all too familiar warning, and read
straight.

Jack:

The church <u>choir</u> met under the lamp to sing carols.
Jack had only ever met *ch* as in *church*, so *choir* caused him
some puzzlement. But despite his lack of phonic cues for *ch*, and the
very strange *oir*, he was brave enough to believe the evidence of
other cues:

- a picture;

- the words *to sing carols*;

- and having *choir* already in his spoken vocabularly.

Rosie:

"Well, <u>we'll</u> be off now".
Rosie first read *"Well well be off now"*.
Her second try replaced the non-sense of *well be* with:
"Well, we will be off now".
Finally, she combined cues from her experience of how people talk
with cues from recent punctuation work in class, to read correctly:
"Well, <u>we'll</u> be off now".

Harry:

Slugs! Mr. Slime was most fond of such very <u>nice</u> food.
At first, Harry read *nasty food* for *nice food* - *nasty* fitted with slugs
and it began with *n*.
However, he had become sufficiently tuned in to the author's tone of
voice to see it was a joke and he went back to re-read it as *nice*.

 **These four successful readers
used a detective-like approach,
based on a BALANCE of cues.**

Kate

knew better than to stop dead at *straight* and painfully struggle to
build it.

Jack

knew to visit a range of cues which overcame the phonic peculiarities
of *choir.*

Rosie and Harry

also had been encouraged to search widely, rather than to stick
within the problem word itself.

**Most young readers need
help to learn this balance.**

The next four chapters show you how to provide that help.

Chapter 2:
Bookbinding: the right way to start

This chapter aims to show you:

- some practical ways to promote detective-like thinking from the very beginning, even before children can read for themselves.

It will help you to understand:

- that for readers to become efficient users of cues they must learn to use them from the very beginning;

- that you are important in building this early foundation.

Early learning about cues from "Bookbinding"

In Chapter 1 we met five competent nine-year-olds - Ben, Kate, Jack, Rosie and Harry - all efficient users of cues.

So, when did they first become aware of cues?

It happened during "Bookbinding", that important early stage when the adult reads and the child shares the book.

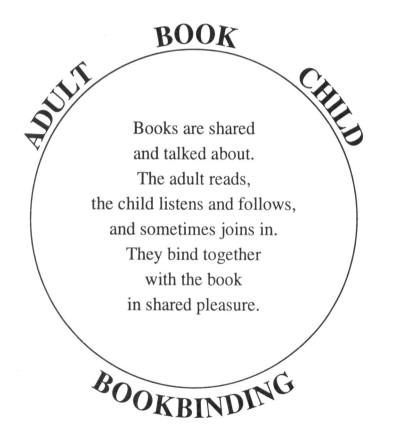

BOOK

ADULT

CHILD

Books are shared
and talked about.
The adult reads,
the child listens and follows,
and sometimes joins in.
They bind together
with the book
in shared pleasure.

BOOKBINDING

Comfortably relaxed within this magic circle, children enjoy their part in the hunt for meaning.

Almost without realising it, they are hard at work, balancing seen and unseen cues.

This is the very foundation of their reading future.

Like any other good foundation, it should be built with care and understanding.

Here are eight practical things you can do when you Bookbind:

1. Read <u>for</u> the child.

2. Help the child to "read between the lines".

3. Help the child to "read beyond the lines".

4. Help the child to take an interest in the look and sounds of words.

5. Help the child to chime in.

6. Spend time reading the pictures.

7. Make the author come alive.

8. Have a good time.

Each suggestion is described more fully on the following pages.

1. Read FOR the child

Mum:	*Grandad's coming for his tea tonight.*
Harry:	*Oh goody! He can read to me again.* *I love his Mr. Wolf voice.*
Mum:	*We'd better shift these papers off the sofa then.* *Give us a hand.*

Reading <u>for</u> the child is the heart of Bookbinding.

When reading for the child the adult is "standing-in" for the author, making the story come alive on the author's behalf.

Interesting and lively reading works best.

- Let the child sit in a position to follow each page.

- Try to read the book beforehand so you can plan a lively reading.

- The meaning is all important, so read in fluent phrases - not ... word ... by ... word.

- Use different voices for different characters.

- Read conversations conversationally - they should sound realistic.

- Use body language and gestures.

- Act out suitable words: shriek when it says 'shrieked', snivel when it says 'snivel' - this is a way for children to learn meanings.

- Explain words which might be new to the child.

- Let your voice show the moods of the story (e.g. panic, delight).

- Speed up and slow down, read loudly and softly, as and when the story demands.

- Pause for effect.

- Build up a sense of expectation as you are about to turn each page.

- Let yourself go; enjoy yourself!

2. Help the child to read between the lines

Mum read: Water was splashing into the puddle from the
              ceiling. It was raining inside the house!

Mum looks puzzled: *Raining inside the house? That can't*
                       be right, can it?

Jack: *Aah! I get it. It's not really raining!*
          A pipe's burst.

Jack read between the lines. The author did not state
outright that a pipe had burst, but Jack added his own
experience to what limited information he had been given.
He made the links, and got to the meaning.

Reading is like joining the dots in a dot-to-dot picture.
The author provides certain chunks of meaning, the dots.
To get the full picture, readers have to make the connections
themselves.

At the Bookbinding stage, young readers need help to read
between the lines.

- While reading the words on the page, weave in brief comments about the meaning. This will signal to the children that reading is about thinking, and not just about getting the words right.

- Also weave in 'ohs' and 'ahs' and similar responses. These alert the child to subtle changes in meaning.

- Emphasise the important points of a story by actions such as:

  pausing;

  using eye contact;

  using laughter;

  changing your tone of voice;

  changing the expression on your face.

- The pictures are a valuable source of extra information. Talk about them when you are helping children to read between the lines.

- The moment you feel comprehension is being lost be willing to make comments or ask questions which will put things right.

- Change the book if necessary. Don't labour on with a book if comprehension is constantly being lost.

3. Help the child to read beyond the lines

Mum read: The bad cat stole a whole string of sausages.

Rosie pointed to the picture:*Those sausages were for a barbecue.*

Mum: *How do you know?*

Rosie: *'Cos the cat couldn't have got them if they'd still been in the fridge. Like we did, we put sausages on a plate for the barbecue.*

Mum: *Oh, I never thought of that. Aren't you clever? That's good thinking.*

Reading beyond the lines means seeing links between what is being read and real life.

It means querying, challenging and commenting on what is being read. It means passing opinions on its quality. It means saying what you feel about it. It is as much a part of reading as the actual reading of the words.

A child trained in this skill becomes a reader who:

- considers
- compares
- recommends
- criticises.

This training begins in Bookbinding, where books are shared and talked about.

- Make sure you include time to talk about the book as you Bookbind - before, during and after the reading.

- Encourage children when they talk about their reading. Listen out for signs that their reading is going beyond the lines, like:
  Sam: *We have one of these at home*
  or Bobbie: *Why didn't they just go through the window?*
  or Phil: *I luv this bit!*
  Praise this type of thinking. Without rushing on, respond with interest and enthusiasm; together you can explore the thought and take it further.

- Also, open up discussion yourself, with two types of "beyond the line" question:
  - questions to do with connecting the book to the child's experience and understanding of life and the world
    Do you remember when our Gran did that?
  - questions to do with evaluating the tale and how the author has told it:
    Which do you like best? This Cinderella book or that one?

4. Help the child to take an interest in the look and sounds of words

Mrs. Betts read:　　Trip trap! TRIP TRAP Daddy goat went over the bridge.

Mrs. Betts:　　*I read that bit really loudly because it's in big capital letters.*

Tracey pointed excitedly to the Tr:　　*That's in my name!*

Mrs. Betts:　　*Well spotted. It starts it, doesn't it?*

Tracey (exploring):　　*Trip, trap, trick, treat …*

Mrs. Betts (joining in her game):　　*Tracey Trouble! Trust tricky Tracey to trot into trouble.*

Detailed knowledge of words starts to form here in Bookbinding. With your help and support, children will:

- build a collection of words known on sight
- begin to understand the make-up of words.

This is important and detailed learning. And yet it can be accomplished in a gentle and fun way if we remember: words so interesting that they are playthings in themselves are excellent tools for learning to look at words; children's natural delight in such words leads them to make links between the way words sound and the way they look.

Children take pleasure in repetition.

- Children love unusual words such as 'didgeriddoo', or 'bommiknocker'. Emphasise these words as you read them, roll them around in your mouth.

- Get the child to say them with you.

- Children love rhyme. Encourage them to spin further rhymes from the words.

- Help children to notice the letter patterns which some rhymes share ('wall-fall').

- Praise children when they spot words with the same letter patterns: "That's in my name - E*mm*a ... tu*mm*y".

- Point to interesting letter patterns as you say them, e.g. double letters ('boo!'; 'bees buzz'), runs of repeated letters ('grrrr!' 'zzzzzz'); and point to capital letters for names.

- Point out when the print is telling you to read differently, e.g. bold, italics, capitals, punctuation marks.

- Be alert to words the children are beginning to recognise, e.g. names, TV slogans, brand names; draw attention to them when they crop up.

- It's OK to use books with some 'long' words. It is often these words which children learn first. (You can have more fun with 'stegosaurus' than 'was').

- Make good use of books which contain lots of repetition. Make sure you point to the repeated phrases as you read them.

5. Help the child to chime in

Grandma read: The third little pig made his house of …

She paused mid-sentence, pointing to a picture that clearly showed bricks.

Pritesh thought about it.

Gran re-read, this time adding the cue br…:
The third little pig made his house of br…

Pritesh chimed in: *Bricks!*

Chiming in tells you that the child is beginning to use cues.

Every contribution children make strengthens their confidence and builds motivation, as they begin to:

- memorise a familiar story or rhyme;
- recognise individual words;
- anticipate rhyme;
- predict a word or words based on the pictures;
- predict a word or words based on the sense.

Furthermore, they tap into what is a huge area of learning:

- matching how words sound with how they look, and vice versa.

34

- Create opportunities for chiming in, by pausing before:

  - a rhyme the child knows well
    (Humpty Dumpty had a great … fall);

  - a new but obvious rhyme
    (one, two, three you see … me);

  - a refrain (ee aye ee aye oh);

  - a repeated phrase
    (who's been sleeping in my … bed?);

  - a punch line
    (… and they never saw her again!);

- Sometimes it helps to hold onto a word, with a question in your voice: He huffed and he…?

- Perhaps include the initial sound of the next word: He huffed and he ppp…?

- Praise children when they chime in of their own accord.

- Any chiming in that differs from the author's words should still be received positively. Simply re-read the author's words correctly, with no hint of criticism, as in this example:

Grandma read: The second little pig made his house of …

Pritesh chimed in: *Wood!*

Grandma: *Yes, it _was_ a sort of wood.*

Grandma re-read: The second little pig made his house of sticks.

6. Spend time reading the pictures

Dad and Trevor were looking at the last picture in 'Where the Wild Things Are', showing Max in his bedroom.

Dad: *Wow! Max <u>did</u> have a long journey.*

Trevor: *No he didn't. It was a dream. Look, there's his supper. If he'd gone missing, his mum would've screamed when she brought it in, and dropped it, probably.*

Then Dad read: … where he found his supper waiting for him.

Trevor: *See! Told you!*

Pictures matter. They are a planned part of the book.
They are often intended to play as vital a role as the words, very often adding an extra layer of meaning.

Pictures hold a fund of cues. These are of value when children "read" stories just from the pictures.
As they interpret the picture cues they experience being in charge of meaning-making.

But of course picture cues continue to be of value when interpreted alongside the adult's reading of the text.

Furthermore, pictures prompt children to revisit pages, and are a key factor in their choosing and re-choosing of a book.

- Encourage children to interpret the story by "reading" the pictures:

  - before you read the book to them;

  - as you read;

  - after you've read the book.

- Build children's confidence and skills by letting them return again and again to "reading" a story from the pictures, with and without adult support.

- As you read, spend time chatting about the pictures - explore them, point things out, dwell on details. Give the child a chance to do the same.

Remember the illustrator!

The next session looks at ways of making
the author come alive. Most of the suggestions
also apply to the illustrator.

7. Make the author come alive

The children of the Reception class showed a great deal of interest when they met a real author. Their questions tumbled out:

Charlie (thinking about his own writing!) *How long does it take you to write a whole book? I mean, do you have to get it right first time?*

Sarah: *Did you tell the stories to your own children?*

Kate: *Have you ever been to the jungle or did you just guess it?*

Ben: *You said pigs eat food from sacks. Well, ours don't.*

Arnold: *Which book do you think is your best? I think, the one about badgers.*

Children need to know that books don't just come "straight from the shops and factories". They need to know they are written by real people, people who think, feel, imagine and observe - all things that children do.

They need to know this basic fact because it will have a huge impact on the way they respond to reading:

- more interested;
- more ready to question;
- more appreciative.

Readers at later stages will need to think in some depth about an author's craft. At this stage we are just laying the foundation.

Whether meeting the author is possible or not, every now and then when you Bookbind spend a little time drawing the child into thinking about the author:

- Use the term 'author', and point out the name on the cover, spine and elsewhere.

- Point out any information about the author, perhaps from the back cover (sometimes there's a picture).

- Watch out for collectable information on authors, in newspapers, magazines and other media, to give you interesting background to talk about with the children.

- Tell the child about other books by the same author. You might be able to collect some of these books together.

- Look for a dedication, and talk about it ("Who could Rob and Rosie be?").

- Get the child used to the idea that an author's book often appears in other forms, e.g. as a film, a video or a TV series. Talking about the differences is a good "beyond the lines" experience.

- Draw attention to those authors who are also their own illustrators.

8. Have a good time

"Have a good time" may seem to be a somewhat light-weight piece of advice for a task as complex as learning to read. Yet it is the most important of all.

It plays a vital part in forming the way children approach learning.

"Having a good time" means:

- lots of reading by the adult for the child;

- genuine interest in the book from both adult and child;

- a warm, relaxed, friendly atmosphere;

- every contribution from the child received with interest and respect;

- mistakes expected and accepted.

"Having a good time" produces children...

- who feel secure to have-a-go; vital, because learning to read is all about learning to solve problems;

- who gain a lasting impression of reading sessions as enjoyable team work;

- who enjoy reading, and want to come back for more.

- Expect to do the lion's share of the reading.

- Encourage contributions - they let you into the child's thinking.

- Never let there be any hint that you are assessing the child.

- Find a comfortable place for Bookbinding.

- If you can, find a quiet, uninterrupted time.

- Create a friendly atmosphere; leave any problems outside the door.

- Don't press on if interest starts to wane. Don't spoil ten enjoyable minutes with a further five spent pushing on too far.

- Be happy to re-read favourite books. Always keep your reading fresh, however well you know the book.

- Let your enthusiasm show. It will be infectious, and help to forge a lifelong love of reading.

Chapter 3:
Working out words

This chapter aims to show you:

- how to move on from Bookbinding as children begin to read more for themselves;

- how to teach children more about cues;

- a 3-point plan to help a reader work out a problem word.

It will help you to:

- value children's detective-like thinking when they are using cues;

- instruct children who are stuck on a problem word so they can;

  - "Focus" on the cues they are already using;

  - "Study" other available cues;

- choose and use Focus Words;

- choose and use Study Words.

As children begin to read more words for themselves, so a different type of adult support is needed.

The almost total support of Bookbinding now gives way to more instruction on what cues are and how to use them.

Your opportunity to provide this instruction comes when a child sticks on a word.

In any one reading session there will usually be a number* of words the child cannot read.

This brings us to the problem that is at the heart of supporting children with their reading:

* There is more about this in Chapter 5.

When to tell a word?

When to work on a word?

Here is a three-point plan to help you at this stage:

In any one reading session…
you should **TELL** most of the words that a child sticks on

you should **FOCUS** attention on 1 or 2 of them

you should **STUDY** 1 quite closely.

TELL

Q.

Why tell most of the problem words when the aim is to help children work words out?

A.

Because telling problem words:

- maintains a good natural pace, important in keeping sessions enjoyable, and building a love of reading;

- encourages fluency as the normal way to read, unlike a word-by-word plod where the beginning of a sentence has been forgotten by its end;

- retains the flow of meaning, providing the information a reader needs for working on Focus and Study words.

**And what are
Focus and Study Words?**

FOCUS

Work on only 1 or 2 Focus Words per session.

A Focus Word is any word that the child has got partly right. Some cues will have been used, but others will have been missed.

Your job with a Focus Word

Point out and praise the cues used.

Point out the cues that have been missed.

Say the whole word, putting it back into the flow of the reading.

Working on a Focus Word:

- highlights the fact that cues exist;

- introduces a range of cues;

- builds the child's confidence.

STUDY

Work on only 1 Study Word per session.

A Study Word is just like a Focus Word, except that the cues missed may be within the child's grasp. If you feel the child could find these cues if pointed in the right direction, you have found your Study Word.

Your job with a Study Word

Point out and praise the cues used.

Guide the child in a search for the cues that have been missed.

Say the whole word, putting it back into the flow of the reading.

Working on a Study Word:

- increases the child's familiarity with cues;

- develops independence in finding and using cues;

- builds the child's confidence.

TELL

FOCUS

STUDY

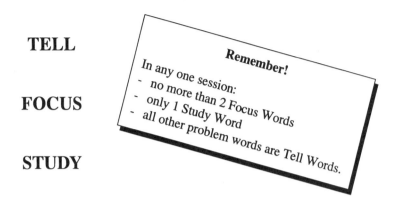

Remember!

In any one session:
- no more than 2 Focus Words
- only 1 Study Word
- all other problem words are Tell Words.

The three point plan in action

The rest of this chapter is given over to watching Kate, Jack, Rosie, Harry and Ben, children met in Chapters 1 and 2, as they are supported in reading sessions at this stage.

We show each child at work on a Focus Word, and then show each tackling a Study Word.

They are shown in a range of situations, either supported by family at home or by Teaching Assistants in school.

Each scene takes up no more than a few minutes of the whole reading session.

How to read each
of the following scenes

Read all through the scenario
on the left hand page first.

It shows what happened
when a child came to a problem word.

Then re-read it in connection
with the comments on the right hand page.

The text that the child is reading is shaded.

Focus Words

No. 1: Kate. Example of a Focus Word - Breakfast

John woke up.
The puppy woke up, too.
Mum called out: *"Breakfast!"*

Teaching Assistant, Mrs. Jaspal: *Oh, I remember John. We've met him already in your other book. Nice cosy picture. Is he getting up or going to bed, do you think? Mmm, there's light coming through the curtains.*

Kate: *I think it's morning.*

Mrs. Jaspal: *Yes, I do. I think he's just waking up. Look, his puppy's just woken up, as well.*

Kate: *I bet the dog woke him up!*

Kate begins to read: John woke up. The puppy woke up, too. Mum...
[she pauses]

Mrs. Jaspal supplies words: called out...

Kate carries on reading: Mum called out...
[Kate pauses to think.]

She hesitantly suggests: *Br ... Is it 'Breakfast'?*

Mrs. Jaspal: *Good thinking. Makes sense – he's just woken up. Let's keep reading and see if we can check it out.*

Kate flicks through the next five pages and finds a picture of a breakfast scene.

Kate: *I was right!*

Mrs. Jaspal: *Course you were! You saw it started with 'Br'. So it certainly wasn't his sssupper!*

Kate: *Yes - and it's morning. You can tell from the pictures.*

50

Breakfast is picked as a Focus Word because:

- Kate had used a phonic cue (*Br...*);
- and a meaning cue (she knew it was morning).

Mrs. Jaspal mentions the name John to save Kate the problem of reading it from cold.
She has recognised the need for 'tuning in', and eases Kate gently into her new book.

Similarly, Mrs. Jaspal uses *waking, woken,* and *as well,* as prompts for woke and too, in the text.

Mrs. Jaspal knows that it is important to keep the story flowing. Frequent halts to work-out problem words can destroy the necessary build-up of context which provides meaning cues. They also remove any sense of relaxed enjoyment. So this time when Kate's pause indicates a problem word, she simply supplies it.

Mrs. Jaspal confirms Kate's guess with a meaning cue.
She hints that there are further meaning cues to be found.

Kate confirms her own guess with a picture cue.

Mrs. Jaspal draws attention to Kate's correct use of a phonic cue.
And Kate understands the help that came from the pictures.

No. 2: Harry. Example of a Focus Word - jumped

Some frogs came in and
jumped on the table.
One was the king.

Harry had read this book at school during Guided Reading in the Literacy Hour. He is reading it again at home with his mum, who is having to supply 1 word in about every 10 words.

Turning the page, he pauses to think about the first word Some .

Mum (points and says the word) Some

Harry: Some frogs came in and
just sat on the table
One was the king.

Mum allowed him to read on to the end of the page, because his alternative *just sat* made a certain sense.

Mum then comments first on the interest of the story: *I love this frog, head first in the cup! That one's the king, look, with the crown on. I wonder who these others are?*

Then Mum comments on Harry's alternative reading: *I can see why you said "just sat" on the table - these four frogs are just sitting. I think you were using these first two letters only: 'ju-'. Fine. But if you split it this way: 'j-ump', then you get a bigger chunk of the word 'jump'.*

She reads, pointing word by word: jumped on the table. *There's no 'sat' at all.*

Harry: *That one's jumped, jumped into the cup!*
He carries on reading, the next page.

jumped is picked as the Focus Word because:

- Harry seems to have sounded *ju-* correctly, but not used the rest of the word's phonics;
- he seems to have over-relied on the cues in the picture, which show frogs sitting, not jumping;
- it gave Mum the chance to show how to tackle **jump** as *j-ump*, and not as *j-u-m-p*.

Note the link between school and home.
It's good to read a book more than once.
This ratio of 1 in 10 is a useful level for working sessions like this.

Mum silently counts to three before calmly saying the word for Harry.

Brilliant! Mum sees that *just sat is* no major loss of meaning, so she doesn't interrupt. Harry reads on to the page end, giving him the chance to go back and correct his mistake for himself.

Mum takes great care that the 'work' of reading will not over-ride the pleasure of the story, the real reason for reading.

Mum talks through Harry's cue-use for him.
Then she supplies one more cue which he had missed.

No. 3: Jack. Example of a Focus Word - pupa

Where is the pupa?
The grubs feed for about twelve days. Then each grub makes a
neat, rounded cocoon out of silk. Can you see some of these
rounded cocoons in the picture? Inside its cocoon each grub
changes into a *pupa*.

The class had watched a TV programme about bees and had been
given a box of 'bee books'. Jack took his choice to a volunteer
helper, with a puzzled look:

Jack: *Mrs Thwaite, where's the puppy in this picture?*

Mrs. Thwaite: *Where does it say that, Jack?*

Jack points to the last word in the heading.

Mrs. Thwaite: *Oh, I can see why you are reading 'puppy'. That first
bit of the word looks like 'pup'. Jack, why is your teacher asking you
to read about bees?*

Jack: *I dunno.*

Mrs. Thwaite: *I think it's going to tell us about what we saw on TV
this morning. I think we'd better read this page together. You start. It
tells about what the grubs do.*

Jack: The grubs feed for about 12 days. Then each grub makes a *nest...*

Mrs. Thwaite: ... a neat, rounded cocoon of ...

Jack: ... silk. Can you see some of these rounded cocoons in the
picture? Inside the cocoon each grub ch- ch-

Mrs. Thwaite: ... changes into a ... *Now, Jack, think about the TV.
Remember the name that was used for what the grubs turn into. Not
p-ŭ-p, but pū-p...?*

Jack: *Pupa!*

Mrs. Thwaite: *That's right. You remember vowels have two sounds.
If one doesn't work, try the other! ŭ as in puppy, no! ū in pupa, yes!*

54

Pupa was picked as a Focus Word because of:

- Jack's use of a phonic cue: *pup...,* and the chance it gave Mrs. Thwaite to make a link with other recent phonic work;
- the chance it gave her to show Jack that the use of prior knowlege is all part of the reading game.

Mrs. Thwaite puts into words the phonics that Jack has used, giving him credit for what he knows. Also she wants Jack to tap into the prior knowledge which she knows he can bring to this problem word.

She is giving him a helpful prompt for the first sentence.

She simply gives the correct version, without stopping to comment. This lets the flow of reading continue, with the build-up of meaning cues that Jack needs. Moreover, she knows the extent of Jack's attention span, and is holding things together until they reach the chosen Focus Word **pupa.**

Mrs. Thwaite is aware of some of Jack's other recent phonic work, when she had shown him the difference between *super* and *supper.*

No. 4: Ben. Example of a Focus Word - carried

I got cold and Mum *carried* me
all the way back.

Dad and Ben are sharing a book at bedtime. It's a book new to both, about a mother and daughter on a moonlit beach.

Ben has been following very well, with Dad reading most of the words, and Ben chiming in. They have read about the little girl's dip in the cold sea, and have reached the point where the pair are returning home.

Ben turns over to this new page. He studies the picture, glances at the words, and says excitedly: *Let me read this bit. I can read this.*

Ben reads: I got cold and Mum *cried* all the way back.

Dad: *Wow! You did read that well. Great. But I tell you what: I think the mum's quite happy, really. Look at her face; I don't see her crying.*

Dad points to carried and says: *But that word certainly does look a bit like 'cried'.*

Dad then re-reads the page, pointing to the picture of the little girl on her mum's back .

Ben repeats sleepily: ... carried me all the way back.

Carried is picked as a Focus Word because:

- Ben's attempt shows some good signs of phonic cue use:
  c...ried/carried;
- it gave Dad the chance to remind Ben that important cues
  come from the pictures as well as the words.

Because this is a new book, and because it is bedtime, Dad is quite prepared to do all the reading, until Ben falls asleep.

However, Dad is only too pleased to give way to Ben's enthusiasm.

Dad praises the good attempt.

This is where Dad points out the cue in the picture. This is much more easily within Ben's reach than the phonics of **carried.**

This is all Dad wants to say about phonics, right now. He knows the phonics of **carried** are just too hard for Ben as yet.

Ben isn't aware that he had ignored **me.** Dad chooses not to mention it, in this relaxed session.

No. 5: Rosie. Example of a Focus Word - greet

One evening when the boys got home from school there was no-one to *greet* them. "Where's Mum?" demanded Mr. Piggott when he got home from work.

Rosie has brought her library book to share with her Grandma. Deeply interested in the pictures, which link closely to the words, Rosie has been reading well, with Grandma supplying 1 word in about every 10. Rosie and Grandma agree that the mum in the story has a miserable life, and Rosie is now on the page which hints at the household changes ahead.

Rosie: One...
Rosie pauses to think about the next word.

Grandma: evening...

Rosie: One evening when the boys got home from school there was no-one there to *meet* them. "Where's Mum?" de- de- dem- [pauses]

Grandma: ... demanded...

Rosie: ... demanded Mr. Piggott when he got home from work.

Grandma: *You read that page really well, Rosie love.*

Rosie: *She's gone! The mum's gone! Serves 'em right.*

Grandma: *Too right. There's no-one there when they get back from school, no-one to meet them, or,* [pointing to the word] greet *them. Look how 'meet' and* greet *are nearly the same, just the beginnings 'gr' and 'm' are different.*

Rosie: *They nearly mean the same, don't they?*

Grandma: *Well, you greet people when you meet them. And the last part of each word is spelled the same, -eet, so you read that bit quite correctly. Go on, turn over now. Let's see what happened to mum. Let's see if you're right.*

greet was picked as a Focus Word because:

- it demonstrated good cue-use: it was largely phonically correct (in fact, the last part of the word, its 'rime', -*eet*, was correct);
- it offered a chance to talk about subtle differences in word meanings.

Grandma supplies the word in order to keep the story flowing along.

Grandma does not intervene. Because *meet* and **greet** are so close in meaning, Grandma lets her carry on right to the end of the page before she mentions Rosie's attempt. This way, she keeps a good balance between developing Rosie's fluency and polishing up her word-attack skills.
Once again Grandma supplies the word in order to keep the story flowing along.

Only now, at this point, does Grandma point out the different 'onsets' of **greet** and *meet*: *gr* and *m*.

And here she points out the rime -*eet*.

Study Words

No. 1: Kate. Example of a Study Word - tie

There was a *tie* on the bed.
The puppy grabbed it.
He tried to eat it.

By now, Kate was nicely into her new book, and her Teaching Assistant had already pointed out to her two Focus Words, but as yet there has not been a Study Word opportunity.

Kate, reading: There was a t-

Mrs. Jaspal: *Keep going, Kate. Keep reading. Keep looking ahead for clues - I mean 'cues'. Let's use the proper word!*

Kate: on the bed [pauses]

Mrs. Jaspal: *Keep going. Get used to going past a full stop.*

Kate: The puppy grabbed it.

Mrs. Jaspal: *Keep going. Can you read the whole page?*

Kate: He tried to eat it.

Mrs. Jaspal: *Now, here's a cue. What is this 'it' that the puppy grabs and tries to eat? Not sure? 'It' is the 'something' on the bed that the puppy grabs - look -* [points to picture] *– and tries to eat*

Kate: *Scarf?*

Mrs. Jaspal: *Yes, it looks very much like a sc-arf. But listen.*
There was a t-

Kate: *Dad's tie!*

Mrs. Jaspal: *Well done, Kate, well done. Right! I'm just going to put* tie *in your reading record. Your mum and dad, and your teacher, will be interested in how you got it. You pulled all the cues together - the picture, all the words, the t- sound.* There was a tie *… Good girl.*

`tie` was picked as a good Study Word because:

- it gave a chance to guide Kate into a hunt for cues through more than one sentence;
- it gave Kate a chance to link picture and meaning cues with her own good cue *'t'*.

Mrs. Jaspal decides not to go down the phonic route because *ie* is new to Kate.

She knows that Kate often needs a push to read on into the next sentence.

Mrs. Jaspal has spotted more cues ahead.

'It' is such an easy word to read, yet children often fail to link it to what it stands for.
She reminds Kate not to overlook the obvious picture cues.

She praises Kate's thinking.

This is where she links all the cues she has talked about to Kate's first cue *'t'*. She makes sure Kate knows what she is going to record. She records how well some cues were used, and, ready for her next exchange with Kate's teacher, the fact that *'ie'* was met but not taught.

No. 2: Harry. Example of a Study Word - Goodbye

The magic key was glowing.
"It's time to go," said Biff.
"Goodbye," said the king.

Harry is nearing the end of his book from school. Mum has talked to him about a couple of Focus Words, and has almost decided there will be no Study Word for tonight.

Then Harry reads: The magic key was glowing.
"It's time to go," said Biff.
"Goody," said the king.

Harry looks up: *Why does he say 'Goody'? Is he glad?*

Mum: *Well, is he glad? Look again at his sad-face! And Biff's. And Gran's.*

Harry: *They look fed-up.*

Mum: *Why are they fed-up? They're at a party on the page before! No need to be fed-up there!*

Harry: *The party's over 'cos the key's glowing.*

Mum: *OK. Now look back at this word. You know the king's speaking because there are these speech marks, and it says* said. *When you said 'Goody' you actually got the beginning of this word beautifully:* Good- *So, what do people say when they are leaving?* Good- *?*

Harry: Goodbye *!*

Mum: *Great! You've got there. You got that new word because you already knew half of it, and you looked at the picture, and you thought about how people feel when they have to leave a party. Come on now, let's see how it ends. Read to the end, and I'm going to put in your record book how much we've both enjoyed this story, and how clever you were, getting 'Goodbye'.*

Goodbye was picked as the Study Word because:

- it gave Mum the chance to guide Harry to the cues he had overlooked;
- it gave Harry the chance to link cues from pictures, meaning and speech-marks, with his own cue *Good-*.

At this stage in the session Harry was comfortable with the book, and tuned-in to thinking about cues, from his Focus Words.

He had realised *Goody* didn't make sense, which shows he was using some meaning cues.

Mum guides him to connect picture cues from two different pages.

Harry is pulling together information from these pictures, and the words, and from his memory of similar magic key adventures.

Mum praises Harry's reading of the first part of the word **Good-** . At the same time she helps him tap into another cue – his knowledge of what people say when they leave.

Mum is consolidating Harry's use of more than one cue, ending the session on a high note. Each time she does this it helps to build his confidence.

Mum writes 'We both enjoyed this story. Harry read *Goody* for **Goodbye,** but we got round it with his general knowledge.'

No. 3: Jack. Example of a Study Word - burrow

The new queen bee is going to dig a *burrow* in the soil. All through the cold winter, the queen sleeps in her burrow.

Jack has become used to his non-fiction book about bees, greatly helped by cues provided by its attractive, strong, colour photographs.

Jack reads: The new queen bee is going to dig a *hole* in the soil. Mrs. Thwaite does not interrupt.

Jack: All through the winter the queen sleeps in her... [he pauses]

Mrs. Thwaite, pointing back to the first time burrow appears: *What did you say for this word?*

Jack: *Did I say 'hole'?*

He points to photograph: *'Cos look, she's going in a hole.*

Mrs. Thwaite: *Have you got any other ideas?*

Jack: *Ermm... nest – could be a nest; look at all this straw.*

Mrs. Thwaite turns the book over: *Think about animals that live underground. What do they live in?*

Jack: *holes...setts...dens...tunnels...*

Mrs. Thwaite: *What about rabbits?*

Jack: *burrows!* He looks puzzled. *Bees in a burrow?*

Mrs. Thwaite turns the book back over again, and reads: The queen bee is going to dig a...

Jack: *It's a burrow. It is burrow.*

Mrs. Thwaite: *That's right. Well done.*

She reads: The queen bee is going to dig a burrow in the soil. *That's how we sometimes read, Jack. We use our own general knowledge and check it out against the word on the page. That surprised you-* burrow. *Look, if I change that 'u' to an 'a', we get 'barrow'. Take the 'b' away and it's 'arrow' ... put 'n' on, and it's 'narrow' ...*

burrow was picked as the Study Word because:

- it gave Mrs. Thwaite the chance to tap into Jack's evident good background knowledge of animals;
- it gave her the chance to show Jack how to move away from picture cues;
- it gave Jack the chance to orchestrate cues from his background knowledge, pictures and phonics.

Mrs. Thwaite waits to see if Jack will self-correct.

She is still hoping for a self-correction.

Now Mrs. Thwaite is tapping into Jack's good background knowledge of animals.

By turning the book over, she moves Jack away from the misleading picture cues, to force him to tap into his own background knowledge. (This book-turning tactic is equally useful for print - whenever the reader becomes fixated on any one single cue to the exclusion of others).

She is refining his use of his background knowledge.

Jack takes his unexpected new knowledge back to the page, where the phonics of the word clinch it for him. Just which bits of the word clinched it we don't know – as is often the case.

She is helping Jack to play with phonics.

No. 4: Ben. Example of a Study Word - promise

Kitten forgot all about her *promise* and went out into the dark to look for Mum.

One Saturday morning Ben picked up his favourite but difficult book and asked Dad to read it for him. A few pages in, Dad read: Suddenly she felt lonely and hungry. She wanted Mum's soft fur and Mum's warm milk.

Ben: *My turn! I'll read:* Kitten ... (he pauses).

Dad: forgot.

Ben: *I can do it! I can do it!* forgot all about her p... p... (pauses).

Dad: *Keep going. Miss it out.*

Ben: and went into the dark to look for Mum. Ben points back to promise. *I know that, 'cos you told it to me before.*

Dad: *Yes, I did. And I reckon if you can build that first bit, you'll get it. Have a go. Go on.*

Ben: p.r.o.m.

Dad: pr-om

Ben: pr-om prom...

Dad: *That's better. Now read it from the beginning again.*

Ben: Kitten forgot all about her prom... all about her prom... promise !

Yeah, 'cos she made this promise to her mum, and she's gonna get attacked by an owl in a minute... Hey, Dad, remember when our Tibby got lost?

promise was picked as the Study Word because:

- it gave Dad the chance to show how building the first part of a word may be all the reader needs;
- its meaning was already on the tip of Ben's tongue.

This next page has fewer lines.

Because Ben knows the story well, Dad hopes the information later in the sentence will trigger the memory of the kitten's **promise**.

Dad realises that quite often part of a word will prompt the rest, given supportive context.

Dad re-shapes Ben's building (p.r.o.m.) into onset and rime (pr-om).

Aware of the dangers of isolated phonic work, Dad gets Ben to replace it into the sentence. By delivering on his promise that Ben would "get it from the first bit", he provides him with a demonstration of practical phonics.

Ben is not only slotting together the whole story line, but also making a connection with real life.

No. 5: Rosie. Example of a Study Word - squealed

"When is Mum coming home?" the boys *squealed* after another horrible meal.
"How should I know?" grunted Mr. Piggott.

Rosie reads: "When is Mum coming home?" the boys *squeaked*...

Grandma decides to let Rosie keep going.

Rosie: ... after another horrible meal.
"How should I know?" grunted Mr. Piggott.

Grandma: grunted! grunted Mr. Piggott!

Grandma makes a grunting noise. Grunted!

Rosie laughs, and also makes a grunting noise. *Oh! He's grunting like a pig! Oh, look! All the pictures have changed. There are pigs everywhere - even the light switches look like pigs!*

For a few moments Rosie and Grandma enjoy looking back through the pictures, finding all the things that have turned 'piggy' - wallpaper, pots and pans, lamps ... Then:

Grandma: *You know you read "squeaked" here? That's a good word for a mouse word. But a pig word could be...?*

Rosie: squealed !

squealed was picked as the Study Word because:

- it gave Grandma the chance to enjoy with Rosie the author's clever use of 'pig' words;
- Rosie had already used a good range of cues for her alternative *squeaked.*

The cues used by Rosie were: most of the word's phonics, plus her awareness that it was a speech word, and that it was a 'whining' word.

Grandma does not choose the straightforward tidying-up phonic option of pointing out a mis-read *k* for an *l*. Instead she opts to lead Rosie into discovering for herself the range of the author's pig jokes. Grandma emphasises **grunted** because she wants Rosie to pick up on the pig words.

By now, Gran knows that because Rosie is in tune with the pig theme, she is ready to bring that information to correct her word.

These five children were fortunate in being supported by adults who understood the technicalities of working words out while not forgetting that reading goes wider than that.

So they:

- carefully observed the cues being used, and talked about them;
- pointed out the cues being overlooked and gave guidance;
- got the balance right between Tell, Focus and Study.

But they also:

- kept the reading fluent and the praise generous;
- took time to read Between the Lines*;
- took time to read Beyond the Lines*;
- shared the enjoyment.

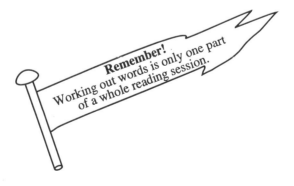

Remember! Working out words is only one part of a whole reading session.

**See Chapter 2, pages 28-31.

Chapter 4:
Ten Useful Actions

This chapter aims to show you how to:

- support readers who, although becoming fluent, still meet the occasional problem word;

- advance the detective-like thinking they began to develop at earlier stages of learning to read;

- ensure that readers get into the habit of using all the cues available.

It will help you to:

- remember ten Useful Actions for when a reader meets a problem word;

- select the best Action for the situation;

- develop self-help skills in the reader.

So there you are, a supportive adult, with a child sitting beside you who is by now reading fairly fluently.

Q.

What are you going to do when he or she comes up against a problem word?

A.

Use one of the following Ten Useful Actions.

Ten Useful Actions
A set of tools for both adult and child

1. Thumb It

2. Hide It

3. Hint At It

4. Take Another Run At It

5. Jump Over It

6. Re-phrase It

7. Make A Question Of It

8. Start It

9. Help to Build It

10. Wait And See

What the ten Useful Actions do

They help readers balance all the cues
Many children seem to get tunnel-vision when faced with a problem word.

They become hypnotised by the letters of the word, ignoring all other cues.

But reading calls for the "orchestration of cues"* - a juggling act of holding meaning in mind while using phonic information.

These ten Useful Actions guide the reader into doing just that.

They help the adult talk about cue use
These Actions help the adult lead the reader into talking about the cues which could solve a problem word.

Such discussion deals with the very nuts and bolts of reading.

It is vital training.

(And no, these Actions won't always lead readers to the "right answer". But they will lead the reader to some very important insights).

In the following pages, each double page describes one Useful Action.
The left-hand pages give examples.
The right-hand pages give explanations.
The text that the child is reading is shaded.

---

*See Chapter 1: How Reading Works (pages 12 & 19).

Useful Action - No. 1
Thumb It

Mum grew more and more *anxious* as darkness fell and still there was no sign of the missing kitten.

Kim: Mum grew more and more ... (long pause, becoming hypnotised by the letters of the word).

Adult: (sensing that the child is not going to read on independently, and seeing the meaning coming up after the word, puts her thumb over the word *anxious*, and reads): Mum grew more and more *something* as darkness fell and still there was no sign of the missing kitten.

Notice that the adult says the word something rather than leaving a gap.

Kim: *Ah, it's like, kind of worried.*

Adult: *You're absolutely right. She would be worried.*

Kim: *Mmm.* (shakes head) *It's not 'worried', is it?*

Adult: *Well, the author could have used that word, so you're half-way there. Now I'll take my thumb away. Look again at the word. It starts with 'a'. Do you know a word that means 'worried' and starts with 'a'?* (re-reads) Mum grew more and more a ......

Kim: anxious

Adult: *Wow! That's brilliant. Funny looking word, isn't it.*

Not all children would know the word *anxious*. If, in this situation, Kim had not come up with it, she would have been told it.

Remember! It's not a crime to tell a word.

What you do

Cover the problem word with your thumb.

Do this from above the word, so as not to hide the next few lines.

Read out the whole sentence to the child, except the problem word.

Say the word *something* in place of the problem word, to keep the sentence flowing.

Read as naturally as possible.

(Don't worry: all this takes seconds only.)

Why "Thumb It" works

Covering the problem word with your thumb draws attention away from the letters of the word and directs it onto wider cues.

This puts children in charge of their own problem-solving.

There is often a lot of help after the word. In our example here, the problem word is sixth in a nineteen word sentence - giving thirteen more words after it to provide more cues.

Useful Action - No. 2
Hide It

We'll look around and then *decide* where you can sleep.

Tony: (Reading very slowly, word by word): We'll. look. a-round. and. then. (pause) d...e...k

Adult: *You're getting too hooked up on single letters again. You're forgetting what the story's about. Now, let's work a bit of magic.* (She turns the book over) *I've turned the book over, so you can't even see the word. But I bet, if I read the whole sentence to you, you can still get close to it. Listen. I'll read it nice and quickly. Listen for the meaning:* We'll look around and then *something* where you can sleep. (Pauses, to give Tony time to think). *It's OK. I'll read it again:* We'll look around and then *something* where you can sleep.

Tony continues thinking, so adult patiently re-reads the sentence a third time: We'll look around and then *something* where you can sleep.

Tony: *Is it 'see'?*

Adult: *Brilliant! Told you you'd get close to it. 'See' is what the author means, but it's not actually 'see'. This time, instead of 'see', he's used 'decide'.* (She turns book back over again, and re-reads the whole sentence, pointing to *decide* as it is read.) *You read it now, Tony.*

Tony: We'll look around and then decide where you can sleep.

Adult: *Excellent.*

Tony has a habit of reading too slowly to hold meaning, so, to avoid too lengthy a break, *decide* was quite simply given. The flow was maintained, and Tony will learn about the phonics later.

What you do

Turn the whole book over, and repeat the whole sentence, saying the word *something* in place of the problem word.

Three or four repetitions may be needed to give the reader sufficient thinking time.

Why "Hide It" works

Turning the book over provides an even bigger break from word-gazing than covering the one single word as in Thumb It.

Like Thumb It, it restores the pace and phrasing of natural language, proving to the child that speed is important.

It temporarily switches the task from a looking-at-words task to a listening-to-the-meaning task.

It is a useful ploy when reading has slowed to a word-by-word pace, and sense has been lost even though each word is read correctly.

Useful Action - No. 3
Hint At It

Mind you, if our *enemies* had been any good they would have finished us off straight away.

Stevie: Mind you, if our en... en... (pause).

Adult: *They're fighting, remember.*

Stevie: ... enemies! ... *yes* ... enemies had been any good they would have finished us off straight away ... (and he continues to read).

What you do

Give a little reminder either about the background, or about what's been read so far.

Why "Hint At It" works

Helping readers recall what has been read so far, or reminding them of the background, are quick ways of making them link meaning with phonics. Such hints need disturb the flow of reading very little.

Brief comments to remind readers of their own personal background knowledge work in the same way: *They've gone angling, don't forget.*

Useful Action - No. 4
Take Another Run At It (Two examples)

▶ Peter rubbed the puppy dry with a *towel* beside the fire.

Max: Peter rubbed the puppy dry with a ... (pause).

Adult: (re-reads) Peter rubbed the puppy dry with aaaa...?
(stressing *rubbed*, *dry* and *with*; holding a rising, questioning note on
a: stopping before *towel*).

Max: towel! *I was thinking that said 'two', but it didn't make sense.*

Adult: *Yes, I can see why you thought that - the same letters are in
there - but I'm glad you realised 'two' didn't make sense.*

▶ I was told it was in here, but I don't know *where*.

Lee: (reading at a word-by-word plod) I. was. told. it. was. in. here.
but. I. don't. know. ... (pause).

Adult: (much more quickly and with
conversational intonation). I was told it was
in here, but I don't know knooow ...? (her voice
rises questioningly on *know*, and she
lengthens the word, to hold it). she re-reads:
I was told it was in here, but I don't knoooow...?

Because he heard a fluent string of words, Lee was able to complete its pattern.

Lee: where ! (and he carries on reading the next sentence).

Adult: *Good* (whispering; hardly interrupting Lee's reading).

What you do

Re-read with natural pace and intonation as far as the problem word, usually from the beginning of the sentence.

Hold and lengthen the word before the problem word, with a questioning note in your voice.

Why "Take Another Run At It" works

Re-reading the sentence as far as the problem word works in two ways:

- first, it helps the reader revalue the meaning of important words in the run up to the problem word (see Max);

- second, it acts as a trigger for the right word; this works even when the cues in the run up seem rather 'colourless' - *it; was; in; here; but; I; don't...* (see Lee).

Useful Action - No. 5
Jump Over It

They hid in the barn and the *deafening* noise of the machine made them unable to hear anything.

Ahmed: They hid in the barn and the dee… (pause).

Adult: *Keep going. Miss it out. You can come back to it.*

Ahmed: (starting again and reading on past the problem word): They hid in the barn and the *something* noise made them unable to hear anything (repeats). They hid in the barn and the *something* noise made them unable to hear anything.

Ahmed has picked up from his teacher the technique of saying the word something in place of the problem word.

Ahmed: *Is it the same as 'loud'?*

Adult: *That's it! It means 'loud'. So you know you're looking for a word that means 'loud'. Now you've got the meaning, let's go back to the letters for some more help.*

Ahmed: deef (pauses) deaf!

Adult: *The deaf noise? Does that fit? And is it long enough? Look at the word* (points to *deafening*). The deaf … noise. *Remember you said it meant 'loud'.*

Ahmed: deafening !

Adult: *Well done! And well done for using 'something' when you jumped over the problem word.*

What you do

Ask the reader to re-read from the beginning of the sentence, to say the word *something* for the problem word, and to read on to the end of the sentence, all at a good pace. Remind the reader that reading at a good pace often helps to get the meaning.

Be prepared to read the sentence yourself, either to demonstrate this Action or to support a weary reader. Read with good intonation and at a natural pace.

Why "Jump Over It" works

As we noticed with Thumb It, there is often a lot of help after the problem word.

By jumping over the problem word and reading on, the reader not only benefits from the run-up, but is also able to make use of the cues in the rest of the sentence.

Reading at a good pace often helps to get at the meaning

Useful Action - No. 6
Re-Phrase It

We were very poor and couldn't *afford* a barn.

Simon: We were very poor and couldn't ... (pause).

Adult: (first of all trying the Jump Over It Action): We were very poor and couldn't *something* a barn.

Simon: We were very poor and couldn't ... (pause).

(The Jump Over It Action hasn't helped here).

Adult: (Now using Re-Phrase It, turns the book over and changes the sentence just slightly): *We were so poor we couldn't something a barn.*

Adult changed very to so and and to we.

Simon: *Buy?*

Adult: *Great! Now you've got the point.* (Turns book back again) *Now look at the word. Look at the opening letters, and listen again: We were so poor we couldn't something a barn.*

Simon: *aff... aff...* afford!

(returns to the text and reads actual sentence).

We were very poor and couldn't afford a barn.

What you do

Re-phrase the run up to the problem word.

Do this as you repeat the sentence, saying the word *something* for the problem word, and reading on to the end of the sentence.

You may need to try various re-wordings.

With luck you'll hit upon the phrasing which will act as the trigger for the reader to come up with the right word.

Importantly, having got the problem word, the reader must return to the page and read the sentence as it is actually written.

If you keep a pad and pencil to hand, a re-phrasing can sometimes be quickly written out for the reader to see as well as hear.

Why "Re-Phrase It" works

Any sentence can be written in a number of ways:

"We were very poor and couldn't afford a barn"
"We were so poor we couldn't afford a barn"
"We were very poor so we couldn't afford a barn"

Sometimes, for some readers, one way will make more sense than another.

Quite often, re-phrasing is needed to turn book language into more everyday language.

Useful Action - No. 7
Make A Question Of It (Two examples)

▶ The present was sitting on the hall table. Sam *thought* about it all day long.

Nat: The present was sitting on the hall table. Sam ... (pauses).

Adult (quietly, and pretending to be too interested in the story to get hooked up on a problem word): *What did Sam think about all day long?* (She is actually giving him the problem word, even though it's in a different form: think/thought).

Nat: *His present.*

Adult: *Yup. So...* (points to word *thought*) *What did Sam think about all day long?* Sam th...

Nat: Sam thought about it all day long.

▶ He saw an old nest, *high* up in the green branches.

Ben: He saw an old nest ... (pauses).

Adult: *Where did he see an old nest?*

(By asking a 'where' question, she leads him to see that the rest of the sentence is about place, or position).

Ben: *Oh!* ... high up in the green branches.

86

What you do

Turn a sentence round into a question.

Use as many words from the sentence as you can.

Why "Make A Question Of It" works

Making a question out of the actual words of the sentence helps in two ways:

- first, it allows you to give the reader a close alternative to the problem word, as with Nat's *think/thought*. Sometimes, you can even plant the actual word into the reader's mind: *What was it that Sam thought about all day long?*

- second, it allows you to point the reader in the right direction (see Ben).

Such a large amount of help keeps the child's confidence high.

It keeps the reading flowing without too much disruption.

Useful Action - No. 8
Start It (Two examples)

▶ She opened the box and *suddenly* a jack-in-the-box popped out!

Fran: She opened the box and s...s...s...

Adult: *Miss that out. Keep going.*

Fran: (distracted by the problem, reading quite flatly) a. jack. in. the. box. popped. out.

Adult: (reads the whole sentence at a normal pace, and builds a part of the problem word). She opened the box and s-ud..., sud... a jack-in-the-box popped out! (repeats) She opened the box and s-ud..., sud... a jack-in-the-box popped out!

Fran: suddenly! ... suddenly a jack-in-the-box popped out.

▶ When his parents asked what he was doing, Mallory replied 'Well, it's *obvious*, isn't it? I'm building a robot'.

Neal: When his parents asked him what he was doing, Mallory replied 'Well, it's...' (pause) *Mmmmmm...* ob... obv... (pause) Well it's obv ... (pause)

Adult: (aware that 'obv' is not a letter-string usually found in English, but not commenting on that) *Good thinking, Neal. I can see you're trying your run-up again, with a clever bit of building so far. Read a bit further, see if that helps.*

Neal: ... 'Well it's obv... isn't it' - obvious' !

What you do

Re-read up to the problem word, and start building it, using one or more of its initial sounds.

If this is not enough to trigger the word, once again re-read up to the word, again build the first part, but this time read on to the end of the sentence.

Why "Start It" works

Using phonics and meaning together in this way is a very good example of what is meant by balancing the cues. Here is the "orchestration of cues" at work.

The phonics is provided by building the beginning of the word.

The meaning is provided by the natural reading of the words around the problem word.

The reader brings both together to clinch the word.

Useful Action - No. 9
Help To Build It

This is a *cardinal* beetle. (a caption to a picture).

James: *I don't know what that says* (pointing to cardinal).

Adult: *Well, what does that say?* (pointing to beetle).

James: beetle.

Adult: *Well now, if that* (pointing to *cardinal*) *is coming in front of 'beetle', it's probably telling us something about it.*

James: *It's its name, I think.*

Adult: *So do I. What kinds of beetle do you know?*

James: *Ladybird... cockroach... don't know any more... Oh! stag beetle?*

Adult: *So... does that say 'stag'? No. Well, here's a new one for you. I think because we have no other cues at all, we'll have to have a go at building this. See anything in there that you know?*

James: car...card...

Adult: *Go on.*

James: card...in...al... card-in-al... cardinAL?

Adult: (re-stressing it) CARdinal. *That's right. Well done.* This is a cardinal beetle. James has learned a fact about beetles via a wholly phonic attack.

Let's say the beetle had been a chilopod, and so beyond James' building skills, then the adult would have told him the word.

Remember! It's not a crime to tell a word.

What you do

Help the child to build the word.

Why "Help To Build It" works

It is useful when meaning cues are hard to find.

It works when the phonics of the word are within the child's grasp.

It can be a way for readers to learn words completely new to them, as James did in our example.

WARNING:
Helping children to build words can be tricky. Make sure your phonic work is in line with what the reader is doing in school.

Useful Action - No. 10
Wait And See

It was his *wicked* uncle who was king at that time. This bad man had sent Ali to prison, where he stayed for many a long day.

Jack: It was his wickt -.

Adult: (does not interrupt).

Jack: - uncle who was king at the time. This bad man had sent Ali to prison, where ... *Ah!* (self-corrects) ... wicked uncle! *I thought 'wickt' didn't make sense.*

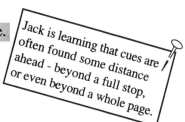

Jack is learning that cues are often found some distance ahead - beyond a full stop, or even beyond a whole page.

(re-reads) It was his wicked uncle who was king at *the* time. ...

Adult: (quickly and unobtrusively, hardly interrrupting) *Well done. You did that yourself. Good.*

Jack: (continues) ... This bad man had sent Ali to prison, where he stayed for many a long day.

(Adult makes note to comment on '...icked' later).

If Jack had not corrected his error himself, then of course the adult would have helped him, using one of the other Useful Actions.

What you do

When children continue reading past a mis-read word, wait, to give them an opportunity to self-correct from information further on in the text.

You will have to decide how long to let the reading go on after the mistake. This will depend on how much it has changed the sense, or lost the meaning. Some mistakes may make hardly any difference at all - king at *the* time/king at *that* time – and you might choose to let them pass completely.

Why "Wait And See" works

Wait And See is not an easy option. The temptation is to jump in as soon as a mistake is made.

But we are working to train children to be independent readers, and the cues to solve a problem word are often further on.

In this example, the adult let Jack keep going over one full stop, and half way into the next sentence; patience which was well rewarded.

**Those were the ten Useful Actions put to work. And the
evidence is clear: meaning backs up phonics, phonics
back up meaning.**

Meaning backs up phonics

Here is a list of all the problem words found in our examples:

anxious	deafening	suddenly
decide	afford	obvious
enemies	thought	cardinal
towel	high	wicked
where		

What would have happened if our readers had been asked to read
these words just as a list? How would they have dealt with them?

They might have recognised as whole words one or two commonly
used words such as *high* or *where* (see Literacy Hour High
Frequency Word Lists).

Otherwise, their only way through would have been to build them -
to use phonic cues in isolation. And in doing that, in most of these
words they would have been hampered by phonic difficulties.

So it is rare for phonics alone to do the trick. However, add context,
as in our examples*, and there are meaning cues to back up the
phonic cues.

* Useful Action 9, Help To Build It, is the one exception.

Phonics back up meaning

But of course, phonic information is vitally important. There is no reading without it.

For instance, if Kim (Action 1, page 74) were to meet a blank space instead of the word *anxious,* the meaning of the sentence would prompt her to come up with a range of alternatives: tense, worried, frightened, fearful, afraid, nervous, scared, anxious…

Try generating a list of alternatives for some of the problem words opposite. You will find they are not huge lists; they are manageable.

Without any letters to guide her, she would have no anchor to hold her to the choice of *anxious.*

And that's why readers need phonic information.

Phonic information can be the starting point. It is also the final checkpoint for all the alternatives prompted by meaning cues.

Phonics and meaning work together

IT'S ALL IN THE BALANCE

Chapter 5:
The three reading levels

Every reader, at whatever stage, always has
THREE READING LEVELS

This chapter aims to show you:

- the three reading levels:
  Independent: books read with ease
  Instructional: books read with support
  Frustration: books to listen to;

- how each level makes a vital contribution to reading development;

- how to vary your help to match the book.

It will help you to:

- make sure children experience all three levels in any one week;

- understand the benefit a reader gets from each level;

- gauge the level of any book for any reader;

- talk to children about their Independent Level books;

- instruct children at their Instructional Level;

- extend children's experience by reading Frustration Level books to them.

The three reading levels

Learning to read requires a balanced diet of three different reading levels. In any one week children should:

1. read easy books for themselves (Independent Level);
2. read medium-difficulty books with adult support (Instructional Level);
3. listen to more difficult books being read to them (Frustration Level).

Let's take one child, Jack, as an example.
(Jack's problem words are shown as ■ ■ ■ ■)

JACK'S INDEPENDENT LEVEL

1. EASY BOOKS
- where nearly all the words can be read

Frog and Toad went out to fly a kite. They went to a large ■ ■ ■ ■ ■ *(meadow)* where the wind was strong. "Our kite will fly up and up," said Frog. "It will fly all the way up to the top of the sky." "Toad," said Frog, "I will hold the ball of string. You will hold the kite and run." Toad ran across the grass. He ran as fast as his short legs could carry him. The kite went up in the air. It fell to the ground with a bump. Toad heard ■ ■ ■ ■ ■ ■ ■ *(laughter)*. Three birds were sitting in a bush.

2. MEDIUM DIFFICULTY BOOKS
- where quite a few words cannot be read

Tim got slowly out of bed. His ■■■■■■ *(throat)* hurt.
When he washed his face, he found that his neck hurt a bit,
too, if he pressed it. Tim pulled on his ■■■■■■■ *(clothes)*.
He must get Sebastian outside before anyone saw him. He
■■■■■■ *(tucked)* a sleepy Sebastian under his jacket. He
was just going downstairs when he remembered the box.
He couldn't leave that in his room. He put Sebastian back
on the bed, and got out an old canvas ■■■■■■■■ *(shoulder)*
bag and slipped it on his ■■■■■■■■ *(shoulder)*. Then he
picked Sebastian up again.

3. DIFFICULT BOOKS
- where very many words cannot be read

… he unbolted the door and was in the act of entering the
sty with a bucket of food when he suddenly saw an old rat
that stood up on its ■■■■■■■ *(hindlegs)* on the wall
and ■■■■■■■■ ■■■■■ *(actually bared)* its yellow
teeth at him in the most ■■■■■■■■ *(impudent)* and
■■■■■■■■■ *(provoking)* manner ■■■■■■■■■■
(imaginable). ■■■■■■■ *(Angrily)* the man looked about
for a stick or stone, but by the time he found something
the rat had vanished. ■■■■■■■ *(Cursing)* the cheek of
the ■■■■■■■■ *(creature)*, he pulled the door shut and fed
the ■■■ *(sow)* and her litter, never ■■■■■■■■■ *(noticing)*
that the ■■■■■ *(tally)* of pushing, shoving, squealing,
gobbling little lords and ladies now numbered only nine.

JACK, LIKE ALL CHILDREN, NEEDS ALL
THREE LEVELS IN ANY ONE WEEK

Children need all three levels

At their Independent Level ...
children can read an easy book for themselves. They enjoy themselves. Not only that, they also practise what they already know about reading, build confidence, and feel they've arrived as readers.

At their Instructional Level ...
children are supported as they read a more difficult book. They receive instruction on how to tackle problem words. They learn just how many cues they can use, from pictures, from printed words, from their knowledge of books and life.

At their Frustration Level ...
children listen to more demanding books. They meet more complex language, which helps them handle more difficult reading material in the future. Also they meet facts, situations and ideas matching their interest level. Such books act like trailers for forthcoming attractions. Through this wider experience, children become hooked on books.

So how can we be sure
which level is which?

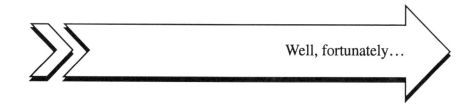

Well, fortunately...

We can measure each level

This is easily done by counting the problem
words in a passage of about 100 words.

<u>INDEPENDENT</u>
0-2 problem words per 100

<u>INSTRUCTIONAL</u>
2-7 problem words per 100

<u>FRUSTRATION</u>
10 or more problem words per 100

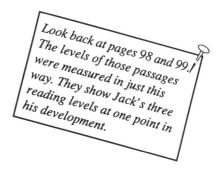

Look back at pages 98 and 99.
The levels of those passages
were measured in just this
way. They show Jack's three
reading levels at one point in
his development.

This method means we can know the level of a particular
passage for a particular child.

For instance, take Rosie, Jack and Kate...

Rosie, Jack and Kate are in the same class. They have very different reading abilities. Given the self-same passage:

- Rosie can read it for herself;

- Jack learns to tackle problem words, with support;

- Kate has to listen to it being read.

INDEPENDENT
LEVEL
FOR ROSIE

Tim got slowly out of bed. His ■ ■ ■ ■ ■ ■ *(throat)* hurt. When he washed his face, he found that his neck hurt a bit, too, if he pressed it. Tim pulled on his clothes. He must get Sebastian outside before anyone saw him. He tucked a sleepy Sebastian under his jacket. He was just going downstairs when he remembered the box. He couldn't leave that in his room. He put Sebastian back on the bed, and got out an old ■ ■ ■ ■ ■ ■ *(canvas)* shoulder bag and slipped it on his shoulder. Then he picked Sebastian up again.

Tim got slowly out of bed. His ■ ■ ■ ■ ■ hurt. When he washed his face, he found that his neck hurt a bit, too, if he pressed it. Tim pulled on his ■ ■ ■ ■ ■ ■ . He must get Sebastian outside before anyone saw him. He ■ ■ ■ ■ ■ a sleepy Sebastian under his jacket. He was just going downstairs when he remembered the box. He couldn't leave that in his room. He put Sebastian back on the bed, and got out an old canvas ■ ■ ■ ■ ■ ■ ■ bag and slipped it on his ■ ■ ■ ■ ■ ■ ■ . Then he picked Sebastian up again.

Tim got ■ ■ ■ ■ ■ ■ out of bed. His ■ ■ ■ ■ ■ ■ hurt. When he ■ ■ ■ ■ ■ ■ his ■ ■ ■ ■ , he ■ ■ ■ ■ ■ that his neck hurt a bit, too, if he ■ ■ ■ ■ ■ ■ ■ it. Tim pulled on his ■ ■ ■ ■ ■ ■ ■ . He must get ■ ■ ■ ■ ■ ■ ■ ■ ■ outside before anyone saw him. He ■ ■ ■ ■ ■ ■ a sleepy Sebastian under his jacket. He was just going downstairs when he ■ ■ ■ ■ ■ ■ ■ ■ ■ the box. He ■ ■ ■ ■ ■ ■ ■ leave that in his room. He put Sebastian back on the bed, and got out an old ■ ■ ■ ■ ■ ■ ■ ■ ■ ■ ■ ■ bag and slipped it on his ■ ■ ■ ■ ■ ■ ■ ■ . Then he picked ■ ■ ■ ■ ■ ■ ■ ■ ■ up again.

The same passage - but three different reading levels...

... and three different types of support

Independent Level –
where nearly all the words can be read

AT THEIR INDEPENDENT LEVEL children can read an easy book for themselves. They enjoy themselves. Not only that, they also practise what they already know about reading, build confidence, and feel they've arrived as readers.

To support children at their Independent Level adults should:

- let them know it's OK to be reading at this level - adults do;

- let them know most of their reading should be at this level;

- show approval of this level by encouraging them to relax and have fun;

- never let "easy book" equal "worthless book";

- trust them to sit and read by themselves at this level;

- make sure there are lots of books at this level, for browsing and choosing;

- organise a place and a time for the child to sit and read undisturbed; encourage this activity;

- talk about the book rather than the child's performance;

- aim to have as much prior knowledge of the book as possible;

- show an interest in the storyline and illustrations;

- ensure that chatting about the book is relaxed and friendly (don't quiz);

- ask more open-ended questions than closed:

  (open-ended = many answers are possible
  e.g.   How else could Billy have escaped?
         Which is your favourite bit about the dog?

  closed question = only one answer possible
  e.g.   Out of which window did Billy escape?
         What was the name of the dog?);

- be careful not to ask questions about every single book.

Instructional Level -
where quite a few words cannot be read

AT THEIR INSTRUCTIONAL LEVEL children are supported as they read a more difficult book. They receive instruction on how to tackle problem words. They learn just how many cues they can use, from pictures, from printed words, from their knowledge of books and life.

To support children at their Instructional Level adults should:

- limit the number of words that are worked on by choosing words -

  - at which the child has made a sensible attempt;

  - which seem to be within the child's grasp;

Look back at Chapters 3 & 4 for the detailed explanation of how to help children tackle problem words.

- tell most of the problem words; there should be more problem words told than worked on, because this -

    - keeps the flow of meaning going (this meaning will directly help the reader tackle the few other problem words chosen for working on);

    - helps word recognition, as the child matches the heard word to the printed word;

    - maintains an enjoyable sense of fluency on these more difficult books;

    - allows more of a book to be read in one session.

NOW LET'S TAKE A CLOSER
LOOK AT THIS LEVEL IN ACTION

The next four pages describe one
particular Instructional Level session.

Tony's previous Instructional Level sessions have moved him on from guessing wildly at unknown words to understanding that the reading game is all about cues.

Further sessions will enable him to find and use cues for himself.

Tony knows that his sessions with Instructional Level books will:

- last no longer than 15 minutes;

- begin with a few minutes of general chat about the book;

- include listening to the previous page read to him as a lead-in;

- have a solid working period in the middle;

- end with some wider discussion about the book as a whole;

- includes lots of praise.

The adult supporting Tony:

- is interested in *how* children attempt to puzzle out problem words;

- gets them to explain their attempts;

- lets this interest over-ride any temptation to demand word-perfection;

- is relaxed about mistakes; realises all learning involves making mistakes;

- realises all learners can learn from their mistakes;

- encourages children to read on after a mistake to give them a chance to self-correct;

- is patient;

- is generous with praise;

- has built up a set of practical ideas for helping children tackle problem words (see Chapters 3 and 4).

Now turn over to see Tony working on four selected problem words.

Tony is reading a page at his Instructional Level

1

Tony halts at *throat*.
Adult gets him to read on to full
stop. This doesn't help.
Adult reads: **His** something **hurt**.
Tony: **His** t...*toe* **hurt**.
Adult: Good. 't' for toe.
But look, and listen. These three
go together: **His thr... hurt**.
Tony: **throat!**

2

Tony reads *plastered it* for
pressed it.
Adult: Good. You read on.
And *plastered* fits with *hurt*
and *it*. Good thinking. But
plastered starts with *pl*.
Tony: *prees...*
Adult: Nearly. Don't forget to try
changing the first vowel sound.
Tony: **if he pressed it**

Tim got slowly out of bed. His ▪▪▪▪▪ *(throat)*
hurt. When he washed his face, he found that his
neck hurt a bit, too, if he ▪▪▪▪▪▪ *(pressed)* it.
Tim pulled on his ▪▪▪▪▪▪ *(clothes)*. He must
get Sebastian outside before anyone saw him. He
▪▪▪▪▪ *(tucked)* a sleepy Sebastian under his
jacket. He was just going downstairs when he
remembered the box. He couldn't leave that in his
room. He put Sebastian back on the bed, and got
out an old ▪▪▪▪▪ *(canvas)* ▪▪▪▪▪▪▪
(shoulder) bag and slipped it on his ▪▪▪▪▪▪▪
(shoulder). Then he picked Sebastian up again.

3

Tony reads *cloth* for
clothes.
Tony: (puzzled) *cloth?*
Adult: It's worth taking
another run at that. Read
again from *Tim*.
Tony re-reads, again
reading *cloth*.
Adult: Sometimes, Tony,
there's a clue in the next
sentence. Tim's going
outside, look. So what
does he need to pull on?
Tony: **his clothes**
Adult: Well done! It was
clō not *clŏ*, wasn't it?

4

Tony reads: **He** touched
a sleepy Sebastian for
He tucked etc.
Adult: Good. *Touched*
makes a kind of sense.
And the word here does
look a lot like *touched*.
But what did the previous
sentence tell us?
Right - he's got to hide
Sebastian. And look at
the picture. Now, look at
the word again.
Tony: Aha! **tucked**

5

Tony was tiring at this
point...
... so the adult told
him *canvas, shoulder*.
Adult considered he'd
worked hard enough.
<u>And</u> there were two
problems together -
three problems in the
one sentence (unlike
one per sentence, so
far). Adult judges this
a step too far... best to
finish on a high note.

The adult supporting Tony managed to:

a) coax him to read on to the end of a sentence;
b) coax him to read on into a new sentence;
c) praise him for reading on;
d) encourage him to read back over a previous sentence;
e) coax him to take a re-run at the word;
f) relate the word to the immediate context;
g) relate the word to the wider context;
h) draw his attention to the picture;
i) relate the word to his background knowledge;
j) give him a phonic cue (he didn't have to build the whole word);
k) repeat the sentence using the word *something* for the problem word;
l) remind him of previous phonic tuition;
m) tell Tony the words when the proportion of hard words shifted the level up to Frustration Level.

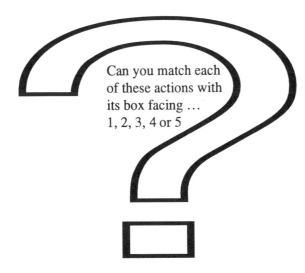

Can you match each of these actions with its box facing …
1, 2, 3, 4 or 5

For answers, see page 114.

Frustration Level -
too hard to read, but not too hard to enjoy

AT THEIR FRUSTRATION LEVEL children listen to more demanding books. They meet more complex language, which helps them handle more difficult reading material in the future. Also they meet facts, situations and ideas matching their interest level. Such books act like trailers for forthcoming attractions. Through this wider experience, children become hooked on books.

To support children at their Frustration Level adults should:

- read these books to them;

- realise that 'frustration' occurs only if children try to read this Level for themselves;

- recognise that, although a listening activity, it still promotes reading development;

- make sure that this 'bedtime-story' type of experience is a regular event;

- understand that this experience is needed throughout all stages of reading development - from very young non-reader to older competent reader;

- see it as a long term investment: the pay-off is in the future;

- make sure children can recognise when a book is at their Frustration Level, and know who to turn to;

- avoid a 'flat' read; make the reading as lively and interesting as possible -

    - shout the shouts, whisper the whispers, shiver the fears, weep the tears...

- have fun, let yourself go: even the mildest attempt to liven up your reading has an effect;

- welcome a wide range of material - fiction, non-fiction, poetry, instructions, history books, science books, magazines, comics ...

- use taped books;

- exploit the two-way links between books and their film/TV versions, between films and their printed spin-offs;

- encourage children to develop their own individual tastes and interests - perhaps exploring one author, or type of book, or theme.

So, three reading levels for our children's balanced reading diet; matched with three very different kinds of adult support

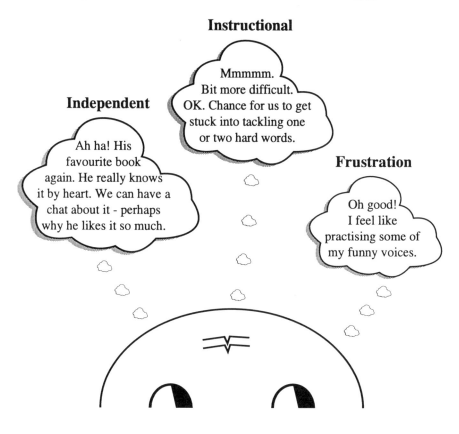

Children, also, need to know about these three levels

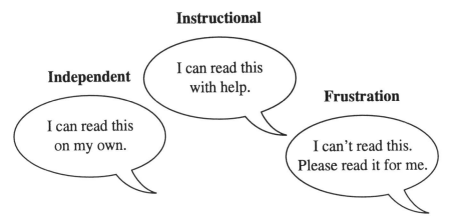

Children, encouraged by adults with a positive and knowledgeable respect for all three levels grow to understand that learning to read is a combination of experiences.

And these are the children who become complete readers.

Note to schools

A child's reading is usually supported by a number of people: some at home, some at school – a potential recipe for confusion. For the child's sake we need a clear system to weld these 'numbers' into a 'team', working with one consistent approach.

To this end some schools have made traffic light bookmarks. These signal to both child and supporting adult the reading level of a particular book for a particular child. Further guidance appears on the backs of the bookmarks.

Independent

I can read this on my own.

Instructional

I can read this with help.

Frustration

I can't read this. Please read it for me.

This straightforward communication system, appearing regularly in the child's book bag, gives teachers:

- a quick and easy means to unify a child's reading team;

- a simple tool to strengthen children's understanding of reading levels.

A traffic light system ensures reading safety

Traffic light bookmarks
Photocopiable templates

Independent

GO

I can read this on my own.

Instructional

CAREFUL

I can read this with help.

Frustration

STOP

I can't read this. Please read it for me.

Traffic light bookmarks
Reverse side: Photocopiable templates

Independent

I can read at least 98 out of every 100 words in this book.

GUIDELINE:
Adult tells any problem words.

Instructional

I'm stuck on about 5 words in every 100 in this book.

GUIDELINE:
Adult either quickly tells every problem word. Or, after discussion with school, adult helps reader use cues to tackle *some* problem words (& tells all the rest).

Frustration

I'm stuck on 10 words or more out of every 100 in this book.

GUIDELINE:
Adult reads. Child listens.

118